French's

GRILLING
AND OTHER FAVORITES

STARTERS & SNACKS

CHICKEN SATAY

Prep Time: 15 minutes • Marinate Time: 30 minutes
Cook Time: 5 minutes

**1 pound boneless skinless
  chicken breast halves
1 recipe Peanut Dip
  (page 4), divided**

**Cucumber slices
Chopped fresh cilantro**

1. Soak 8 (6-inch) bamboo skewers in hot water 20 minutes. Cut chicken lengthwise into 1-inch-wide strips; thread onto skewers.

2. Place skewers in large shallow glass dish. Pour *½ cup* Peanut Dip over chicken, turning to coat evenly. Cover and marinate in refrigerator 30 minutes.

3. Place skewers on oiled grid and discard any remaining marinade. Grill over high heat 5 to 8 minutes or until chicken is no longer pink, turning once. Place on serving platter. Serve with cucumber, cilantro and remaining Peanut Dip.

Makes 8 appetizer or 4 main-dish servings

Chicken Satay and Peanut Dip (page 4)

PEANUT DIP

Prep Time: 10 minutes

⅓ cup peanut butter
⅓ cup FRENCH'S® Dijon
   Mustard
⅓ cup orange juice
1 tablespoon chopped
   peeled fresh ginger
1 tablespoon honey

1 tablespoon FRANK'S®
   Original REDHOT®
   Cayenne Pepper Sauce
1 tablespoon teriyaki baste
   and glaze sauce
2 cloves garlic, minced

Combine peanut butter, mustard, juice, ginger, honey, RedHot® sauce, teriyaki and garlic in large bowl. Refrigerate until ready to serve.

Makes 1 cup dip

SPICY MUSTARD KIELBASA BITES

Prep Time: 15 minutes • Cook Time: 10 minutes

1 pound whole kielbasa or
   smoked Polish sausage
1 cup FRENCH'S® Deli
   Brown Mustard

¾ cup honey
1 tablespoon FRANK'S®
   Original REDHOT®
   Cayenne Pepper Sauce

1. Place kielbasa on grid. Grill over medium heat 10 minutes or until lightly browned, turning occasionally. Cut into bite-sized pieces; set aside.

2. Combine mustard and honey in large saucepan. Bring to a boil over medium heat. Stir in kielbasa and RedHot® sauce. Cook until heated through. Transfer to serving bowl. Serve with party toothpicks.

Makes 8 servings

PINEAPPLE–SCALLOP BITES

Prep Time: 25 minutes • Cook Time: 6 minutes

½ cup FRENCH'S® Dijon
   Mustard
¼ cup orange marmalade
1 cup canned pineapple
   cubes (24 pieces)
12 sea scallops (8 ounces),
   cut in half crosswise

12 strips (6 ounces)
   uncooked turkey
   bacon, cut in half
   crosswise*

1. Soak 12 (6-inch) bamboo skewers in hot water 20 minutes. Combine mustard and marmalade in small bowl. Reserve *½ cup* mixture for dipping sauce.

2. Hold 1 pineapple cube and 1 scallop half together. Wrap with 1 bacon strip. Thread onto skewer. Repeat with remaining pineapple, scallops and bacon.

3. Place skewers on oiled grid. Grill over medium heat 6 minutes, turning frequently and brushing with remaining mustard mixture. Serve hot with reserved dipping sauce.   *Makes 6 servings*

*Or, substitute regular bacon for turkey bacon. Simmer in enough boiling water to cover; 5 minutes and drain well before wrapping scallops.

SPICY APRICOT SESAME WINGS

Prep Time: 15 minutes • Marinate Time: 20 minutes
Cook Time: 25 minutes

⅓ cup FRANK'S® Original
  REDHOT® Cayenne
  Pepper Sauce
¼ cup FRENCH'S® Dijon
  Mustard
2 tablespoons Oriental
  sesame oil

1 tablespoon red wine
  vinegar
½ cup apricot jam
2 pounds chicken wings,
  split and tips discarded
2 tablespoons toasted
  sesame seeds*

1. Stir RedHot® sauce, mustard, sesame oil and vinegar in small measuring cup. Spoon ¼ cup RedHot® sauce mixture and apricot jam into blender or food processor. Cover; process until smooth. Reserve for basting and dipping sauce.

2. Place wings in large bowl. Pour remaining RedHot® sauce mixture over wings; toss to coat. Cover; marinate in refrigerator 20 minutes.

3. Place wings on oiled grid and discard any remaining marinade. Grill over medium heat 25 to 30 minutes or until crispy and no longer pink, turning often. Brush with ¼ cup of the sauce during last 10 minutes of cooking. Place wings on serving platter; sprinkle with sesame seeds. Serve with remaining sauce.   *Makes 8 servings*

To toast sesame seeds, place on baking sheet and bake at 375°F 8 to 10 minutes or until golden.

Spicy Apricot Sesame Wings

CAJUN CHICKEN NUGGETS & GRILLED FRUIT

Prep Time: 20 minutes • Marinate Time: 20 minutes
Cook Time: 20 minutes

½ cup beer or
   non-alcoholic malt
   beverage
¼ cup FRENCH'S® Deli
   Brown Mustard
2 tablespoons oil
1 pound boneless skinless
   chicken breasts, cut
   into 1½-inch pieces
¾ cup plain dry bread
   crumbs

1 tablespoon *plus*
   1 teaspoon prepared
   Cajun seasoning blend
1 pineapple, peeled, cored
   and cut into ½-inch-
   thick rings
2 peaches, cut into 1-inch-
   thick wedges

1. Combine beer, mustard and oil in large bowl. Add chicken pieces; toss to coat evenly. Cover and marinate in refrigerator 20 minutes.

2. Preheat oven to 350°F. Coat baking sheet with nonstick cooking spray. Combine bread crumbs and cajun seasoning in pie plate. Remove chicken from marinade; roll in bread crumb mixture to coat. Discard any remaining marinade. Place on prepared baking sheet. Bake 20 minutes or until chicken is lightly golden brown and no longer pink in center, turning once. Remove to serving plate.

3. Coat fruit with nonstick cooking spray. Place fruit on oiled grid. Grill 5 to 8 minutes over medium heat until just tender. Serve with chicken nuggets and Peachy Mustard Glaze (page 62).   *Makes 4 servings*

*Cajun Chicken Nuggets & Grilled Fruit
and Peachy Mustard Glaze (page 62)*

FRENCH'S® DEVILISH EGGS

Prep Time: 40 minutes • Chill Time: 30 minutes

12 hard-cooked eggs, cut in
   half
6 tablespoons low-fat
   mayonnaise
2 tablespoons FRENCH'S®
   Mustard (any flavor)

¼ teaspoon salt
⅛ teaspoon ground red
   pepper

1. Remove yolk from egg whites using teaspoon. Press yolks through sieve with back of spoon or mash with fork in medium bowl. Stir in mayonnaise, mustard, salt and pepper; mix well.

2. Spoon or pipe yolk mixture into egg whites. Arrange on serving platter. Garnish as desired. Cover; chill in refrigerator until ready to serve.
Makes 12 servings

ZESTY VARIATIONS:

Stir in one of the following:
- 2 tablespoons minced red onion *plus* 1 tablespoon horseradish
- 2 tablespoons pickle relish *plus* 1 tablespoon minced fresh dill
- 2 tablespoons *each* minced onion and celery *plus* 1 tablespoon minced fresh dill
- ¼ cup (1 ounce) shredded Cheddar cheese *plus* ½ teaspoon FRENCH'S® Worcestershire Sauce.

French's® Devilish Eggs

GRILLED QUESADILLA SNACKS

Prep Time: 30 minutes • Cook Time: 2 minutes

1½ cups (6 ounces) shredded
Monterey Jack cheese
½ red or yellow bell pepper,
chopped
2 ounces sliced smoked
ham, cut into thin
strips
2 ounces sliced smoked
turkey, cut into thin
strips

¼ cup finely chopped green
onions
⅓ cup FRENCH'S® Classic
Yellow® Mustard
2 teaspoons ground cumin
10 flour tortillas (6 inch)

1. Combine cheese, bell pepper, ham, turkey and onions in medium bowl. Combine mustard and cumin in small bowl; mix well.

2. Place tortillas on sheet of waxed paper. Spread 1 rounded teaspoon mustard mixture over each tortilla. Sprinkle cheese mixture evenly over mustard mixture. Top with another tortilla, pressing down firmly to form quesadilla.

3. Place quesadillas on oiled grid. Grill over medium heat 2 minutes or until cheese is melted and heated through, turning once. Cut each quesadilla into quarters. Serve with salsa and cilantro, if desired.

Makes 10 servings

Grilled Quesadilla Snacks

HAWAIIAN RIBS

Prep Time: 10 minutes • Cook Time: 40 minutes

1 can (8 ounces) crushed
pineapple in juice,
undrained
⅓ cup apricot jam
3 tablespoons FRENCH'S®
Classic Yellow®
Mustard

1 tablespoon red wine
vinegar
2 teaspoons grated peeled
fresh ginger
1 clove garlic, pressed
3 to 4 pounds pork baby
back ribs*

1. Combine crushed pineapple with juice, apricot jam, mustard, vinegar, ginger and garlic in blender or food processor. Cover and process until very smooth.

2. Place ribs on oiled grid. Grill ribs over medium heat 40 minutes or until ribs are no longer pink near bone. Brush ribs with portion of pineapple sauce mixture during last 10 minutes of cooking. Cut into individual ribs to serve. Serve remaining sauce for dipping.

Makes 8 servings (1½ cups sauce)

*Or, if baby back ribs are not available, substitute 4 pounds pork spareribs, cut in half lengthwise. Cut spareribs into 3- to 4-rib portions. Cook 20 minutes in enough boiling water to cover. Grill ribs 30 to 40 minutes or until no longer pink near bone, brushing with portion of pineapple mixture during last 10 minutes.

 NOTE:

Try mixing 2 tablespoons FRENCH'S® mustard, any flavor, with ¾ cup peach-apricot sweet 'n' sour sauce to create a delicious luau fruit dip. Serve with assorted cut-up fresh fruit.

Hawaiian Ribs

VEGETABLES &

SIDES

GRILLED ASPARAGUS AND NEW POTATOES

Prep Time: 15 minutes • Cook Time: 16 minutes

1 pound small red
   potatoes, scrubbed
   and quartered
¼ cup FRENCH'S® Classic
   Yellow® or Dijon
   Mustard
3 tablespoons minced fresh
   dill *or* 2 teaspoons
   dried dill weed

3 tablespoons olive oil
3 tablespoons lemon juice
1 tablespoon grated lemon
   peel
⅛ teaspoon black pepper
1 pound asparagus,
   washed and trimmed

1. Place potatoes and *¼ cup water* in shallow microwavable dish. Cover and microwave on HIGH (100%) 8 minutes or until potatoes are crisp-tender, turning once. Drain.

2. Combine mustard, dill, oil, lemon juice, lemon peel and pepper in small bowl. Brush mixture on potatoes and asparagus. Place vegetables in grilling basket. Grill over medium-high heat 8 minutes or until potatoes and asparagus are fork-tender, turning and basting often with mustard mixture. *Makes 4 servings*

Grilled Asparagus and New Potatoes

HOME–STYLE BAKED BEANS

Prep Time: 10 minutes • Cook Time: 25 minutes

1 large green or red bell
   pepper, chopped
1 small onion, chopped
2 strips uncooked bacon,
   finely chopped
3 cans (16 ounces each)
   pork and beans

½ cup brown sugar
½ cup FRENCH'S® Classic
   Yellow® Mustard
½ cup FRENCH'S®
   Worcestershire Sauce

1. Place bell pepper, onion and bacon in microwavable 3-quart bowl. Cover loosely with waxed paper. Microwave on HIGH (100%) 5 minutes or until bacon is partially cooked.

2. Stir in remaining ingredients. Microwave, uncovered, on HIGH 20 minutes or until heated through and mixture is slightly thickened, stirring twice. Top with chopped peppers, if desired.

Makes 8 to 10 servings

OVEN DIRECTIONS:

Sauté bacon and vegetables in large nonstick skillet until bacon is cooked; transfer to casserole. Stir in remaining ingredients. Bake at 400°F 45 to 50 minutes, stirring occasionally.

Home-Style Baked Beans

ZESTY GRILLED POTATOES WITH LEMON AIOLI SAUCE

Prep Time: 10 minutes • Cook Time: 20 minutes

4 medium russet potatoes
½ teaspoon salt
⅓ cup melted butter or
margarine
3 tablespoons FRENCH'S®
Dijon Mustard

3 tablespoons FRENCH'S®
Worcestershire Sauce
Lemon Aioli Sauce
(recipe follows)

1. Cut potatoes lengthwise into ½-inch-thick slices. Place potatoes, *1 cup water* and salt in shallow microwavable baking dish. Cover and microwave on HIGH (100%) 10 minutes or until potatoes are crisp-tender, stirring halfway through cooking. (If necessary, cook potatoes in two batches.) Drain.

2. Combine butter, mustard and Worcestershire in small bowl. Brush on potato slices. Place potatoes on oiled grid. Grill over medium-high heat 8 to 10 minutes or until potatoes are fork-tender, turning and basting often with butter mixture. Serve with Lemon Aioli Sauce.

Makes 4 servings

LEMON AIOLI SAUCE

Chill Time: 1 hour

½ cup regular or reduced-
fat mayonnaise
3 tablespoons FRENCH'S®
Dijon Mustard

1 tablespoon lemon juice
½ teaspoon grated lemon
peel
1 clove garlic, minced

Combine mayonnaise, mustard, lemon juice, lemon peel and garlic in medium bowl. Cover and chill in refrigerator 1 hour.

Makes about ¾ cup sauce

GRILLED LEEKS WITH ORANGE

Prep Time: 15 minutes • Cook Time: 7 minutes

6 large leeks
⅓ cup fresh orange juice
3 tablespoons FRENCH'S®
  Deli Brown Mustard
2 tablespoons reduced-
  sodium soy sauce
1 tablespoon olive oil

1 tablespoon FRANK'S®
  Original REDHOT®
  Cayenne Pepper Sauce
2 teaspoons grated orange
  peel
1 teaspoon sugar

1. Trim off all but 1 inch green portion from leeks; discard green tops. Trim off and discard roots. Cut leeks in half lengthwise. Rinse well under cold running water to remove sand between leaves, taking care not to separate leaves from root end.

2. Place leeks and ¼ *cup water* in shallow microwavable dish. Cover with vented plastic wrap and microwave on HIGH (100%) 2 minutes or until leeks are crisp-tender, turning once. Drain.

3. Combine orange juice, mustard, soy sauce, oil, RedHot® sauce, orange peel and sugar in small bowl. Brush mixture on leeks. Place leeks in grilling basket. Grill over medium-high heat 5 to 8 minutes or until leeks are tender and golden brown, turning and basting often with mustard mixture.   *Makes 4 to 6 servings*

GRILLED SWEET POTATOES

Prep Time: 15 minutes • Cook Time: 18 minutes

4 medium-sized sweet
   potatoes (2 pounds),
   peeled
⅓ cup FRENCH'S® Dijon
   Mustard
2 tablespoons olive oil

1 tablespoon minced fresh
   rosemary *or* 1 teaspoon
   dried rosemary
½ teaspoon salt
¼ teaspoon black pepper

1. Cut potatoes diagonally into ½-inch-thick slices. Place potatoes and *1 cup water* in shallow microwavable dish. Cover with vented plastic wrap and microwave on HIGH (100%) 6 minutes or until potatoes are crisp-tender, turning once. (Cook potatoes in two batches, if necessary.) Drain well.

2. Combine mustard, oil, rosemary, salt and pepper in small bowl; brush on potato slices. Place potatoes on oiled grid. Grill over medium-high heat 5 to 8 minutes or until potatoes are fork-tender, turning and basting often with mustard mixture.
    Makes 4 servings

> *French's* **TIP:** The task of selecting sweet potatoes is an easy one. Just look for medium-sized potatoes with thick, dark orange skins that are free from bruises. Sweet potatoes keep best in a dry, dark area at about 55°F. Under these conditions they should last about 3 to 4 weeks.

Grilled Sweet Potatoes

OLD–FASHIONED CORN RELISH

Prep Time: 10 minutes • Cook Time: 2 minutes • Chill Time: 30 minutes

⅓ cup cider vinegar
2 tablespoons sugar
1 tablespoon cornstarch
3 tablespoons FRENCH'S®
   Classic Yellow®
   Mustard
¼ teaspoon seasoned salt
1 package (9 ounces)
   frozen corn, thawed
   and drained

½ cup chopped celery
½ cup chopped red bell
   pepper
¼ cup minced red onion
3 tablespoons sweet pickle
   relish

1. Combine vinegar, sugar and cornstarch in large microwavable bowl; stir until well blended. Add mustard and salt. Microwave, uncovered, on HIGH (100%) 1 to 2 minutes or until thickened, stirring once.

2. Add corn, celery, bell pepper, onion and pickle relish; toss well to coat evenly. Cover and chill in refrigerator 30 minutes before serving.

3. Serve as relish on hamburgers, hot dogs or as a side for barbecued beef or poultry. *Makes about 3 cups relish*

CHEESY BAKED POTATOES

Prep Time: 15 minutes • Cook Time: 50 minutes

1 package (32 ounces) frozen hash brown potatoes, divided	2 cups (8 ounces) shredded Cheddar-Monterey Jack cheese, divided
2 cups milk	¼ cup FRENCH'S® Dijon Mustard
1 package (1.3 ounces) rosy-colored Parmesan pasta sauce mix	3 green onions, chopped

1. Preheat oven to 400°F. Spray 13×9×2-inch baking dish with nonstick cooking spray. Sprinkle half of potatoes in baking dish.

2. Combine milk and sauce mix in medium saucepan. Bring to a boil. Reduce heat; cook 4 minutes or until slightly thickened, stirring often. Remove from heat. Add *1 cup* cheese, mustard and green onions; stir until cheese melts. Pour half of sauce over potatoes. Repeat layers with remaining potatoes and sauce. Cover tightly with foil.

3. Bake 50 minutes or until center is heated through. Uncover; stir. Top with remaining cheese.

Makes 10 servings

> **French's TIP:** Casserole may be baked in disposable foil pan. To reheat: cover and place on grill over low heat until heated through.

SAVORY
SALADS

SPINACH & GRAPEFRUIT SALAD

Prep Time: 25 minutes • Cook Time: 10 minutes

1 bag (10 ounces) spinach,
    washed, stemmed and
    torn
2 cups sliced mushrooms
½ of a red onion, sliced into
    thin wedges
6 slices uncooked bacon,
    cut into thin strips
2 teaspoons cornstarch

½ cup cider vinegar
3 tablespoons sugar
3 tablespoons FRENCH'S®
    Deli Brown Mustard
1 teaspoon FRENCH'S®
    Worcestershire Sauce
2 pink grapefruits, peeled
    and cut into sections

1. Place spinach in large salad bowl. Add mushrooms and onion; set aside. Cook bacon in large nonstick skillet over medium-high heat until bacon is crisp. Drain; reserve 2 tablespoons drippings in pan.

2. Combine *½ cup water* and cornstarch in 2-cup measure until blended. Stir in vinegar, sugar, mustard and Worcestershire. Pour into skillet with bacon drippings. Bring to a boil; simmer 2 minutes or until thickened, whisking constantly. Cool slightly. Top salad with bacon and grapefruit. Pour dressing over salad; toss well to coat evenly. Serve immediately.

Makes 6 to 8 servings

Spinach & Grapefruit Salad

TARRAGON–DIJON CHICKEN SALAD

Prep Time: 30 minutes • Cook Time: 12 minutes
Chill Time: 30 minutes

CREAMY TARRAGON–DIJON DRESSING

2 tablespoons olive oil
1 large shallot, finely minced
1 large clove garlic, pressed
2 tablespoons minced fresh tarragon *or* 1 teaspoon dried tarragon leaves, crushed

½ cup water
⅓ cup reduced-fat sour cream
⅓ cup reduced-fat mayonnaise
⅓ cup FRENCH'S® Dijon Mustard
¼ teaspoon salt
⅛ teaspoon black pepper

CHICKEN SALAD

1 pound small red potatoes, scrubbed and quartered
½ teaspoon salt
1 pound bag mixed gourmet baby lettuce

1 pound prepared rotisserie-style chicken, sliced
1 pint cherry tomatoes, quartered

1. Heat oil in small saucepan over low heat. Add shallot and garlic; cook and stir until just tender. Remove from heat and stir in tarragon. Whisk in remaining dressing ingredients. Cover and chill in refrigerator.

2. Place potatoes and salt in 2-quart microwavable baking dish. Add enough water to cover potatoes. Cover and microwave on HIGH (100%) 10 to 12 minutes or until potatoes are fork-tender, stirring once. Rinse with cold water and drain. Cool completely.

3. Place salad greens on large serving platter. Arrange potatoes, chicken and tomatoes over salad greens. Serve with Creamy Tarragon-Dijon Dressing. *Makes 4 main-dish servings (1½ cups dressing)*

Tarragon-Dijon Chicken Salad

PREMIER POTATO SALAD

Prep Time: 30 minutes • Chill Time: 1 hour

1½ pounds small red
   potatoes, quartered
⅓ cup olive oil
¼ cup FRENCH'S® Deli
   Brown or Classic
   Yellow® Mustard
3 tablespoons lemon juice
¼ teaspoon black pepper

1 cup diagonally sliced
   celery
1 bell pepper (green, red or
   yellow) cut into strips
2 green onions, thinly
   sliced
¼ cup minced fresh parsley

1. Cook potatoes in enough salted boiling water to cover 15 minutes or until slightly tender. Rinse with cold water and drain.

2. Combine oil, mustard, lemon juice and black pepper in large bowl. Add potatoes, celery, bell pepper, onions and parsley; toss well to coat evenly. Cover; refrigerate 1 hour before serving.   *Makes 8 servings*

ORANGE & BEET SALAD

Prep Time: 30 minutes • Chill Time: 30 minutes

2 cans (14½ ounces each)
   sliced beets, drained
2 oranges, peeled and cut
   into sections
½ of a red onion, cut into
   ⅛-inch wedges
2 teaspoons grated orange
   peel

¼ cup FRENCH'S® Dijon
   Mustard
3 tablespoons red wine
   vinegar
1 tablespoon olive oil
1 tablespoon honey
¼ teaspoon salt
¼ teaspoon black pepper

1. Place beets, oranges, onion and orange peel in large bowl. Set aside.

2. Whisk mustard, vinegar, oil, honey, salt and pepper in small bowl. Pour over beet mixture. Toss well to coat evenly. Cover and chill in refrigerator 30 minutes before serving.   *Makes 6 side-dish servings*

PESTO PASTA SALAD

Prep Time: 20 minutes • Chill Time: 1 hour

2 cups firmly packed,
   washed fresh basil
1 cup firmly packed,
   washed fresh parsley
¼ cup slivered almonds
¼ cup (1 ounce) grated
   Parmesan cheese
3 cloves garlic, coarsely
   chopped
½ cup FRENCH'S® Dijon
   Mustard

1 tablespoon FRENCH'S®
   Worcestershire Sauce
⅔ cup olive oil
4 cups cooked, chilled
   small pasta (about
   ½ pound uncooked)
Diced red bell peppers or
   tomatoes

1. Place basil, parsley, almonds, Parmesan and garlic in food processor; cover. Process until finely chopped. Add mustard and Worcestershire; process until well blended.

2. Gradually add oil in slow steady stream, processing until thick sauce forms.

3. Toss pasta with pesto sauce to coat evenly. Top with diced peppers or tomatoes. Cover; chill in refrigerator until ready to serve.

Makes 6 servings (about 2 cups sauce)

 **VARIATIONS:**

Serve pesto sauce as a dip with fresh vegetable crudités or:
• Use as a sauce for gourmet pizzas.
• Toss with cooked, cubed potatoes
   instead of pasta.
• Add to salad dressings.
• Stir into soups.
• Add to quick breads or muffins.
• For a savory herbed garlic bread, spread onto crusty bread
   and grill until toasted.

FRENCH'S® FAVORITE MACARONI SALAD

Prep Time: 20 minutes • Chill Time: 30 minutes

8 ounces uncooked medium shell pasta
⅓ cup reduced-fat sour cream
⅓ cup reduced-fat mayonnaise
⅓ cup FRENCH'S® Deli Brown Mustard

1 tablespoon cider vinegar
3 cups bite-sized fresh vegetables, such as tomatoes, peppers, carrots and celery
¼ cup minced green onions

1. Cook pasta according to package directions using shortest cooking time; rinse with cold water and drain.

2. Combine sour cream, mayonnaise, mustard and vinegar in large bowl. Add pasta, vegetables and green onions. Toss gently to coat evenly. Season to taste with salt and pepper. Cover; chill in refrigerator 30 minutes. Stir before serving.   *Makes 6 (1-cup) servings*

 **NOTE:**

Create German-style mustard by adding minced garlic to FRENCH'S® Deli Brown Mustard.

Top to bottom: Premier Potato Salad (page 30) and French's® Favorite Macaroni Salad

GRILLED BEEF CAESAR SALAD

Prep Time: 20 minutes • Marinate Time: 30 minutes
Cook Time: 17 minutes

1 pound flank steak
1 bottle (8 ounces) Caesar
  salad dressing
⅓ cup FRENCH'S® Dijon
  Mustard
¼ cup lemon juice
1 tablespoon grated lemon
  peel

4 anchovy fillets, rinsed
  and patted dry
  (optional)*
8 thickly cut slices French
  bread
8 cups washed and torn
  romaine lettuce leaves
1 ripe tomato, chopped

1. Place steak in large resealable plastic food storage bag. Combine Caesar dressing, mustard, lemon juice and peel in 2-cup measure; mix well. Pour ⅔ *cup* mustard mixture over steak. Seal bag; marinate in refrigerator 30 minutes.

2. Place anchovies and ¼ *cup* mustard mixture in food processor. Reserve remaining mustard mixture for dressing. Process until very smooth. Brush bread slices on both sides with anchovy mixture. Grill bread over high heat 2 minutes or until lightly toasted on both sides. Set aside.

3. Place steak on oiled grid, reserving marinade. Grill over high heat 10 to 15 minutes for medium-rare, basting frequently with marinade. *Do not baste with marinade during last 5 minutes of cooking.* Let steak stand 5 minutes. Place lettuce and tomato on serving platter. Slice steak diagonally; arrange over lettuce and tomato. Serve with reserved dressing and anchovy bread slices.   *Makes 4 servings*

*Anchovies may be omitted. Brush bread slices with mustard mixture; proceed as above.

Grilled Beef Caesar Salad

3 BEAN & VEGGIE SALAD

Prep Time: 20 minutes • Chill Time: 1 hour

1 can (15¼ ounces) red
    kidney beans, drained
    and rinsed
1 can (15¼ ounces)
    garbanzo beans,
    drained and rinsed
1 package (9 ounces)
    frozen cut green
    beans, thawed and
    drained
½ cup thinly sliced carrots
½ cup thinly sliced celery
½ cup thinly sliced red
    onion

½ cup olive oil
¼ cup FRENCH'S® Classic
    Yellow® Mustard
3 tablespoons chopped
    fresh dill *or*
    2 teaspoons dried dill
    weed
2 tablespoons lemon juice
1 teaspoon sugar
¾ teaspoon salt
⅛ teaspoon black pepper

1. Combine beans, carrots, celery and onion in large bowl. Whisk oil, mustard, dill, lemon juice, sugar, salt and pepper in small bowl until well blended.

2. Pour dressing over beans and vegetables; toss well to coat evenly. Cover; chill in refrigerator 1 hour before serving.

Makes 6 (1-cup) side-dish servings

ASIAN GRILLED CHICKEN SALAD

Prep Time: 30 minutes • Marinate Time: 20 minutes
Cook Time: 8 minutes

1 pound boneless skinless
chicken breast halves,
cut in half lengthwise
⅓ cup FRENCH'S® Dijon
Mustard
3 tablespoons soy sauce
2 tablespoons Oriental
sesame oil
½ cup orange juice or
apricot nectar
2 tablespoons rice wine
vinegar
2 teaspoons grated peeled
fresh ginger

¾ pound asparagus,
washed and trimmed
4 green onions, trimmed
1 yellow or red bell pepper,
cut into thin strips
2 plums, cut into thin
wedges
1 bunch washed and torn
watercress *or* 3 cups
mixed torn greens
½ cup chopped cashews

1. Place chicken in large resealable plastic food storage bag. Combine mustard, soy sauce and sesame oil in 1-cup measure. Pour *⅓ cup* mustard mixture over chicken. Seal bag; marinate in refrigerator 20 minutes. Combine remaining mustard mixture with orange juice, vinegar and ginger; mix well. Reserve for dressing.

2. Place chicken, asparagus and onions on oiled grid. Grill 8 minutes over medium-high heat or until chicken is no longer pink in center and asparagus and onions are tender, turning often. Cool slightly. Cut chicken and vegetables into bite-sized pieces.

3. Place chicken and grilled vegetables in large bowl. Add yellow bell pepper and plums. Pour reserved dressing over all; toss well to coat evenly. Arrange watercress on serving platter; mound salad over watercress. Sprinkle with cashews. *Makes 4 servings*

SANDWICHES &
BREADS

CALIFORNIA TURKEY BURGERS

Prep Time: 15 minutes • Cook Time: 15 minutes

1 pound ground turkey
½ cup finely chopped
   cilantro
⅓ cup plain dry bread
   crumbs
3 tablespoons FRENCH'S®
   Classic Yellow®
   Mustard
1 egg, beaten

½ teaspoon salt
¼ teaspoon black pepper
8 thin slices (3 ounces)
   Monterey Jack cheese
½ red or yellow bell pepper,
   seeded and cut into
   rings
4 hamburger buns

1. Combine turkey, cilantro, bread crumbs, mustard, egg, salt and pepper in large bowl. Shape into 4 patties, pressing firmly.

2. Place patties on oiled grid. Grill over high heat 15 minutes or until no longer pink in center. Top burgers with cheese during last few minutes of grilling. Grill pepper rings 2 minutes. To serve, place burgers on buns and top with pepper rings. Serve with additional mustard, if desired.

Makes 4 servings

California Turkey Burger

MEDITERRANEAN GRILLED FOCACCIA

Prep Time: 20 minutes • Stand Time: 30 minutes
Cook Time: 20 minutes

1 pound frozen bread
dough, thawed and at
room temperature
½ cup chopped walnuts or
shelled pistachio nuts,
toasted
⅓ cup raisins or pitted
oil-cured black olives
1 tablespoon plus
1 teaspoon chopped
fresh rosemary or dried
rosemary

2 teaspoons grated orange
peel
3 tablespoons FRENCH'S®
Classic Yellow®
Mustard, divided
Cornmeal
Olive oil

1. Knead bread dough, walnuts, raisins, rosemary and orange peel on lightly floured surface until well combined. Gradually knead in *2 tablespoons* mustard, adding additional flour as necessary to prevent dough from sticking.* Shape dough into 12×8-inch rectangle.

2. Sprinkle baking sheet with cornmeal. Place dough on baking sheet and sprinkle with cornmeal. Cover with damp towel. Let stand in warm place 30 minutes.

3. Generously brush 1 side of dough with oil. Place on well-oiled grid. Grill over medium-low heat 10 minutes or until bottom is golden brown. Mix remaining *1 tablespoon* mustard with *1 tablespoon* oil; brush over top of dough. Turn dough over; grill 10 minutes longer or until golden brown and cooked through. Cool slightly. Tear into pieces to serve.

Makes 8 servings

*To knead mustard into bread dough, flatten dough to 8-inch circle. Brush with 1 tablespoon mustard. Fold dough in half and knead. Repeat with additional 1 tablespoon mustard.

SOUTHERN BARBECUE SANDWICH

Prep Time: 15 minutes • Marinate Time: 20 minutes
Cook Time: 25 minutes

1 pound boneless sirloin or flank steak*

SOUTHERN BARBECUE SAUCE
½ **cup ketchup**
½ **cup light molasses**
¼ **cup FRENCH'S® Classic Yellow® Mustard**
¼ **cup FRENCH'S® Worcestershire Sauce**

½ **cup FRENCH'S® Worcestershire Sauce**

2 **tablespoons FRANK'S® Original REDHOT® Cayenne Pepper Sauce**
½ **teaspoon hickory salt**
Sandwich buns

1. Place steak in large plastic food storage bag. Pour ½ cup Worcestershire over steak; seal bag. Marinate in refrigerator 20 minutes.

2. Combine ketchup, molasses, mustard, ¼ cup Worcestershire, RedHot® sauce and hickory salt in medium saucepan. Bring to a boil over medium heat. Reduce heat; cook 5 minutes or until slightly thickened, stirring occasionally. Set aside.

3. Place steak on grid. Grill over high heat 15 minutes, turning once. Let steak stand 5 minutes. Cut steak into thin slices; stir into barbecue sauce. Cook until heated through, stirring often. Serve on sandwich buns. *Makes 4 servings*

*Leftover sliced steak may be substituted. Stir into sauce and heat through. Or, substitute 1 pound pork tenderloin for steak. Cook pork until meat is no longer pink.

KIELBASA & KRAUT HEROES

Prep Time: 20 minutes • Cook Time: 20 minutes

1 tablespoon vegetable oil
2 large red onions, cut in
  half lengthwise and
  thinly sliced
2 pounds kielbasa, thickly
  sliced
2 pounds sauerkraut,
  rinsed and well drained
1 can (12 ounces) beer or
  nonalcoholic malt
  beverage

½ cup FRENCH'S® Deli
  Brown Mustard
1 tablespoon caraway
  seeds
8 hot dog or hero-style
  buns

1. Heat oil in large nonstick skillet over medium heat. Add onions; cook 5 minutes or just until tender, stirring often. Remove from skillet.

2. Add kielbasa to skillet; cook and stir 5 minutes or until lightly browned. Drain well. Stir in sauerkraut, beer, mustard and caraway seeds. Cook over low heat 10 minutes or until most of liquid is absorbed, stirring occasionally. Serve in buns.   *Makes 8 servings*

French's **TIP:** This recipe may be prepared ahead. To reheat, place mixture in 12×9-inch disposable foil pan; cover. Place on grid; cook over medium heat 15 minutes, stirring occasionally.

Kielbasa & Kraut Hero

GREEK ISLAND SHRIMP PITA POCKETS

Prep Time: 25 minutes • Marinate Time: 15 minutes
Cook Time: 10 minutes

1 pound large raw shrimp, shelled and deveined
½ cup Italian salad dressing
3 tablespoons FRENCH'S® Deli Brown Mustard
2 tablespoons fresh lemon juice
2 teaspoons grated lemon peel
1 teaspoon dried oregano, crumbled
⅛ teaspoon black pepper
2 tablespoons reduced-fat sour cream

1 cup chopped seeded cucumber
1 cup chopped plum tomatoes
2 green onions, thinly sliced
½ cup (2 ounces) crumbled feta cheese
Olive oil-flavored nonstick cooking spray
4 pita bread rounds

1. Place shrimp in large resealable plastic food storage bag. Combine dressing, mustard, lemon juice, lemon peel, oregano and pepper in 2-cup measure; mix well. Reserve *2 tablespoons* marinade; pour remaining marinade over shrimp. Seal bag; marinate in refrigerator 15 minutes. Stir sour cream into reserved marinade; cover and refrigerate.

2. Toss cucumber, tomatoes, onions and feta cheese in medium bowl; set aside.

3. Thread shrimp onto 4 (6-inch) metal skewers. Place skewers on grid. Grill over medium heat 10 minutes or until shrimp are opaque, turning often. Spray pitas lightly on both sides with nonstick cooking spray; grill 1 minute or until brown on both sides.

4. To serve, cut one-third off tops of pitas; discard. Fill pitas evenly with cucumber mixture. Spoon sour cream mixture over cucumber mixture. Serve pitas with shrimp skewers. *Makes 4 servings*

BISTRO BURGERS WITH BLUE CHEESE

Prep Time: 15 minutes • Cook Time: 15 minutes

1 pound ground turkey or beef	¼ teaspoon dried thyme leaves
¼ cup chopped fresh parsley	2 ounces blue cheese, cut into 4 squares (about 1½ × ¼-inch thick)
2 tablespoons minced chives	Lettuce and tomato slices
2 tablespoons FRENCH'S® Dijon Mustard	4 crusty rolls, split in half

1. Gently combine turkey, parsley, chives, mustard and thyme in large bowl. Divide meat evenly into 8 portions. Shape each into thin patty, about 3 inches in diameter. Place 1 piece cheese between 2 patties, firmly pressing edges together to seal.

2. Place patties on oiled grid. Grill over medium-high heat 15 minutes or until no longer pink. Arrange lettuce and tomatoes on bottom halves of rolls. Top with burgers and top halves of rolls. Serve with additional mustard, if desired. *Makes 4 servings*

GRILLED RATATOUILLE SANDWICH

Prep Time: 25 minutes • Cook Time: 5 minutes

⅓ cup olive oil
⅓ cup FRENCH'S® Deli
   Brown Mustard
1 tablespoon chopped
   fresh rosemary *or*
1 teaspoon dried
   rosemary
3 cloves garlic, minced
½ cup kalamata olives,
   pitted and chopped

½ of a small eggplant
   (about ¾ pound)
1 medium zucchini
1 large red onion
2 large ripe plum tomatoes
1 large red bell pepper
1 (12-inch) sourdough
   baguette, cut
   lengthwise in half
   (about 12 ounces)

1. Combine oil, mustard, rosemary and garlic in small bowl. Place olives in food processor; add *2 tablespoons* mustard mixture. Cover and process until smooth; set aside. Reserve remaining mustard mixture.

2. Cut eggplant and zucchini lengthwise into ¼-inch-thick slices. Cut onion and tomatoes crosswise into ½-inch-thick slices. Cut red bell pepper lengthwise into 2-inch-wide pieces; discard seeds. Place vegetables on platter. Baste with reserved mustard mixture.

3. Place vegetables on oiled grid or vegetable basket. Grill over medium-high heat 3 to 5 minutes or until vegetables are tender, basting and turning once.

4. To serve, remove and discard excess bread from bread halves. Spread olive mixture on cut surfaces of bread. Layer vegetables on bottom half of bread; cover with top half. Cut crosswise into 4 portions.

Makes 4 servings

OLIVE TAPENADE DIP: Combine 1½ cups (10 ounces) kalamata olives, pitted; 3 tablespoons *each* olive oil and FRENCH'S® Deli Brown Mustard; 1 teaspoon minced dried rosemary and 1 clove garlic in food processor. Process until puréed. Serve with vegetable crudités. Makes about 1 cup dip.

*Grilled Ratatouille Sandwiches
and Olive Tapenade Dip*

MAIN–COURSE
MEALS

SOUTH SEAS SHRIMP & MANGO

Prep Time: 15 minutes • Marinate Time: 20 minutes
Cook Time: 7 minutes

1 pound raw jumbo shrimp,
  shelled and deveined
3 tablespoons FRENCH'S®
  Dijon Mustard
2 tablespoons olive oil
2 tablespoons fresh orange
  juice
1 tablespoon FRANK'S®
  Original REDHOT®
  Cayenne Pepper Sauce

1 teaspoon grated orange
  peel
1 large ripe mango, peeled
  cut into 1-inch pieces
1 red bell pepper, cut into
  1-inch pieces
4 green onions, cut into
  1½-inch pieces

1. Place shrimp in large resealable plastic food storage bag. Combine mustard, oil, juice, RedHot® sauce and orange peel in small bowl; pour over shrimp. Seal bag; marinate in refrigerator 20 minutes.

2. Alternately thread shrimp, mango, bell pepper and onions onto 4 (10-inch) metal skewers. Place skewers on oiled grid. Grill over high heat 7 minutes or until shrimp are opaque, turning and basting once with mustard mixture. Discard any remaining marinade.

Makes 4 servings

South Seas Shrimp & Mango

GRILLED APPLE–STUFFED PORK CHOPS

Prep Time: 20 minutes • Cook Time: 40 minutes

**5 tablespoons FRENCH'S®
Deli Brown Mustard,
divided**

**3 tablespoons honey,
divided**

**1 cup corn bread
stuffing mix**

**1 small McIntosh apple,
peeled, cored and
chopped**

¼ cup minced onion

**¼ cup chopped fresh
parsley**

**4 rib pork chops, cut
1¼ inches thick
(about 2 pounds)**

1. Combine ¼ cup water, 2 tablespoons mustard and 1 tablespoon honey in medium bowl. Add stuffing mix, apple, onion and parsley; toss until crumbs are moistened. Combine remaining 3 tablespoons mustard and 2 tablespoons honey in small bowl; set aside for glaze.

2. Cut horizontal slits in pork chops, using sharp knife, to make pockets for stuffing. Spoon stuffing evenly into pockets. Secure openings with toothpicks.

3. Place pork chops on oiled grid. Grill over medium heat 40 to 45 minutes until no longer pink near bone, turning often. Baste chops with reserved glaze during last 10 minutes of cooking.   *Makes 4 servings*

Grilled Apple-Stuffed Pork Chop

CHICKEN WITH PINEAPPLE–MUSTARD SAUCE

Prep Time: 15 minutes • Marinate Time: 1 hour
Cook Time: 45 minutes

1 chicken (3½ pounds), cut into eighths, skin removed
1 can (20 ounces) crushed pineapple packed in juice, drained, reserve juice
¼ cup FRENCH'S® Deli Brown Mustard
1 tablespoon honey
1 tablespoon FRANK'S® Original REDHOT® Cayenne Pepper Sauce
2 cloves garlic, minced
½ teaspoon dried thyme leaves, crushed
2 teaspoons cornstarch

1. Place chicken in large resealable plastic food storage bag. Combine pineapple juice, mustard, honey, RedHot® sauce, garlic and thyme in 2-cup measure. Reserve ⅔ cup pineapple mixture for Pineapple-Mustard Sauce. Pour remaining mixture over chicken. Seal bag; marinate in refrigerator 1 hour.

2. Place chicken on well-oiled grid. Grill over medium heat 45 minutes or until no longer pink near bone, basting occasionally with marinade. *Do not baste during last 10 minutes of cooking.* Discard any remaining marinade.

3. To make Pineapple-Mustard Sauce, combine pineapple, reserved pineapple juice mixture, *¼ cup water* and cornstarch in medium saucepan. Bring to a boil. Cook and stir 1 to 2 minutes or until sauce thickens. Serve chicken with Pineapple-Mustard Sauce.

Makes 4 servings

LONDON CITY BROIL WITH ONION MARMALADE

Prep Time: 20 minutes • Marinate Time: 1 hour
Cook Time: 30 minutes

2 pounds top round steak
½ cup balsamic vinegar or
red wine vinegar
¼ cup olive oil
¼ cup FRENCH'S® Deli
Brown Mustard

2 cloves garlic, pressed
½ teaspoon salt
½ teaspoon black pepper

ONION MARMALADE
¼ cup butter or margarine
4 medium red onions,
thinly sliced
⅓ cup FRENCH'S® Deli
Brown Mustard

¼ cup balsamic vinegar or
red wine vinegar
¾ teaspoon salt

1. Place steak in large resealable plastic food storage bag. Combine
½ cup vinegar, oil, *¼ cup* mustard, garlic, *½ teaspoon* salt and pepper in
small bowl. Pour over steak; turn steak to coat evenly. Seal bag and
marinate in refrigerator 1 hour.

2. To prepare Onion Marmalade, melt butter in large skillet over
medium-high heat. Add onions; cook until very tender, stirring
constantly. Add *⅓ cup* mustard, *¼ cup* vinegar and *¾ teaspoon* salt. Cook
over medium-low heat until mixture thickens, stirring often.

3. Place steak on grid, reserving marinade. Grill over high heat 15
minutes for medium-rare or to desired doneness, turning and basting
often with marinade. *Do not baste during last 5 minutes of cooking.* Slice
steak diagonally into thin pieces and serve with Onion Marmalade.

Makes 8 servings

CAROLINA–STYLE BARBECUE CHICKEN

Prep Time: 15 minutes • Marinate Time: 1 hour
Cook Time: 10 minutes

**2 pounds boneless skinless
chicken breast halves
or thighs**
**¾ cup packed light brown
sugar, divided**
**¾ cup FRENCH'S® Classic
Yellow® Mustard**
½ cup cider vinegar

**¼ cup FRANK'S® Original
REDHOT® Cayenne
Pepper Sauce**
2 tablespoons vegetable oil
**2 tablespoons FRENCH'S®
Worcestershire Sauce**
½ teaspoon salt
¼ teaspoon black pepper

1. Place chicken in large resealable plastic food storage bag. Combine
½ cup brown sugar, mustard, vinegar, RedHot® sauce, oil,
Worcestershire, salt and pepper in 4-cup measure; mix well. Pour *1 cup*
mustard mixture over chicken. Seal bag; marinate in refrigerator 1 hour
or overnight.

2. Pour remaining mustard mixture into small saucepan. Stir in
remaining *¼ cup* sugar. Bring to a boil. Reduce heat; simmer 5 minutes
or until sugar dissolves and mixture thickens slightly, stirring often.
Reserve for serving sauce.

3. Place chicken on well-oiled grid, reserving marinade. Grill over high
heat 10 to 15 minutes or until chicken is no longer pink in center, turning
and basting once with marinade. *Do not baste during last 5 minutes of
cooking.* Discard any remaining marinade. Serve chicken with reserved
sauce. *Makes 8 servings*

Carolina-Style Barbecue Chicken

TUNA KABOBS WITH RED PEPPER RELISH

Prep Time: 25 minutes • Marinate Time: 15 minutes
Cook Time: 8 minutes

1 pound tuna steak, cut
    into 1-inch squares
6 tablespoons red pepper
    jelly*
⅓ cup FRENCH'S® Deli
    Brown Mustard
2 tablespoons balsamic or
    red wine vinegar
½ teaspoon cracked black
    pepper

¼ teaspoon salt
1 red bell pepper, minced
1 green onion, minced
1 orange, unpeeled, cut
    into 1-inch pieces
1 green bell pepper, cut
    into 1-inch pieces

1. Place tuna in large resealable plastic food storage bag. Combine jelly, mustard, vinegar, black pepper and salt in 1-cup measure. Pour ½ cup jelly marinade over tuna. Seal bag; marinate in refrigerator 15 minutes.

2. Combine remaining jelly marinade, red bell pepper and onion in small serving bowl. Reserve for relish.

3. Alternately thread tuna, orange, and green bell pepper onto 4 (12-inch) metal skewers. Place skewers on oiled grid. Grill over medium-low heat 8 to 10 minutes or until fish is opaque, but slightly soft in center, turning and basting halfway with marinade.** Serve with red pepper relish. *Makes 4 servings*

*If red pepper jelly is unavailable, combine 6 tablespoons melted apple jelly with 1 tablespoon FRANK'S® Original REDHOT® Cayenne Pepper Sauce. Mix well.

**Tuna becomes dry and tough if overcooked. Watch carefully while grilling.

Tuna Kabobs with Red Pepper Relish

COUNTRY GLAZED RIBS

Prep Time: 10 minutes • Marinate Time: 1 hour
Cook Time: 45 minutes

**3 to 4 pounds pork baby
back ribs, split
½ cup FRENCH'S® Deli
Brown Mustard
½ cup packed brown sugar
½ cup finely chopped onion
¼ cup cider vinegar**

**¼ cup FRENCH'S®
Worcestershire Sauce
1 tablespoon mustard seed
1 teaspoon ground allspice
Honey Mustard Dip
(recipe follows)**

1. Place ribs in shallow nonmetal baking pan or large resealable
plastic food storage bag. Combine mustard, sugar, onion, vinegar,
Worcestershire, mustard seed and allspice in small bowl. Pour marinade
over ribs, turning to coat all sides. Cover and marinate in refrigerator
1 hour or overnight.

2. Place ribs on oiled grid. Grill over medium heat 45 minutes or until
meat is no longer pink near bone, turning and basting often. *Do not
baste during last 10 minutes of cooking.* Discard any remaining marinade.
Serve with Honey Mustard Dip. *Makes 4 to 6 servings*

HONEY MUSTARD DIP

**½ cup FRENCH'S® Deli
Brown Mustard**

½ cup honey

Combine mustard and honey in small bowl. Cover and refrigerate until
ready to serve. *Makes 1 cup dip*

BARBECUE HONEY–CURRIED CHICKEN

Prep Time: 20 minutes • Marinate Time: 15 minutes
Cook Time: 35 minutes

**3 pounds cut-up chicken,
skin removed
¼ cup FRENCH'S® Dijon
Mustard**

**2 tablespoons honey
2 tablespoons FRENCH'S®
Worcestershire Sauce
2 teaspoons curry powder**

1. Place chicken in shallow dish. Combine mustard, honey, Worcestershire and curry powder in small bowl. Pour half of the curry mixture over chicken, rubbing mixture into chicken. Reserve remaining curry mixture for basting. Marinate 15 minutes.

2. Place chicken on well-oiled grid. Grill chicken, bone-side-down, over medium-low heat 35 minutes or until no longer pink near bone, turning and basting often with reserved curry mixture. *Do not baste during last 5 minutes of cooking.* Discard any remaining marinade.

Makes 4 servings

TIP: You may substitute pork chops or Cornish game hens for chicken.

PEPPERED STEAK WITH DIJON SAUCE

Prep Time: 10 minutes • Cook Time: 15 minutes

4 boneless beef top loin or New York strip steaks, cut 1 inch thick (about 1½ pounds)
1 tablespoon FRENCH'S® Worcestershire Sauce
Crushed black pepper
⅓ cup mayonnaise

⅓ cup FRENCH'S® Dijon Mustard
3 tablespoons dry red wine
2 tablespoons minced red *or* green onion
2 tablespoons minced fresh parsley
1 clove garlic, minced

1. Brush steaks with Worcestershire and sprinkle with pepper to taste; set aside. To prepare Dijon sauce, combine mayonnaise, mustard, wine, onion, parsley and garlic in medium bowl.

2. Place steaks on grid. Grill steaks over high heat 15 minutes for medium-rare or to desired doneness, turning often. Serve with Dijon sauce.   *Makes 4 servings*

TIP: Dijon sauce is also great served with grilled salmon and swordfish. To serve with fish, substitute white wine for red wine and minced dill for fresh parsley.

Peppered Steak with Dijon Sauce

SWEET 'N' SMOKY BBQ SAUCE

Prep Time: 5 minutes

½ cup ketchup
⅓ cup FRENCH'S® Deli
  Brown Mustard
⅓ cup light molasses

¼ cup FRENCH'S®
  Worcestershire Sauce
¼ teaspoon liquid smoke or
  hickory salt (optional)

Combine ketchup, mustard, molasses, Worcestershire and liquid smoke, if desired, in medium bowl. Mix until well blended. Brush on chicken or ribs during last 15 minutes of grilling.   *Makes about 1½ cups sauce*

PEACHY MUSTARD GLAZE

Prep Time: 5 minutes

¾ cup peach preserves
¼ cup FRENCH'S® Classic
  Yellow® Mustard

2 tablespoons orange juice

Microwave preserves in small microwavable bowl on HIGH (100%) 2 minutes or until melted, stirring once. Stir in mustard and juice.

Makes 1 cup glaze

TIP: Brush glaze on chicken, turkey or pork during last 15 minutes of grilling. Serve any extra glaze on the side for dipping.

Sweet 'n' Smoky BBQ Sauce